Original title:
Woodland Wonderings

Copyright © 2025 Creative Arts Management OÜ
All rights reserved.

Author: Seraphina Caldwell
ISBN HARDBACK: 978-1-80567-043-8
ISBN PAPERBACK: 978-1-80567-123-7

Shadows of Ancient Pines

Beneath the boughs where whispers creep,
Mice plot their snacks while badgers sleep.
A squirrel in shades plays hide and seek,
While owls roll eyes, just feeling bleak.

Raccoons in masks do prance around,
Daring the foxes to stand their ground.
Each canopy holds tales to spill,
As shadows stretch, an ancient thrill.

A Symphony of Squirrels

A chorus of chattering fills the air,
As squirrels dance round without a care.
Their cheeks stuffed full of acorn delight,
They giggle and leap from morning till night.

They tease the crows with tricks and pranks,
While rabbits watch from leafy banks.
Every leap and bound sparks a cheer,
In their nutty world, there's no room for fear.

The Language of Falling Leaves

Leaves twirl down in colors bright,
Whispering secrets of day and night.
A leaf says 'hi' as it tickles my nose,
While the grumpy old pine just says, 'Who knows?'

They gossip about the blustery winds,
And laugh at the trees as the season thins.
Caught in a swirl, they dance and they spin,
Each drop a burst of nature's grin.

Twilight Revelations

When dusk descends on critter's spree,
A skunk tells jokes that get a 'Whee!'
The fox rolls over, hardly amused,
At tales of squirrels and acorns used.

A raccoon leads a moonlit parade,
While fireflies twinkle, not one afraid.
Under the stars, they sing and they sway,
In the twilight realm, it's all just play.

Canopy Conversations

Squirrels chatter in the trees,
Debating nuts, or just say 'cheese!'
Birds take bets on who will fall,
While leaves just rustle, having a ball.

A raccoon sneaks with stealthy flair,
Claims the prize—now who would dare?
Frogs croak jokes, the ants just sigh,
As mushrooms giggle, oh my, oh my!

Beneath the Boughs

Beneath the branches, shadows dance,
A hedgehog prances, what a chance!
The mushrooms whisper, 'Here comes the chef!'
They laugh at the clumsy rabbit's misstep.

The mice have a party, cheese in the air,
While owls roll eyes, 'It's too loud to bear!'
A fox in a cape declares with a grin,
'I'm the best dancer, let the fun begin!'

Flora's Silent Song

Flowers gossip in a colorful row,
'Who's the prettiest? Do you know?'
The daisies twirl, the roses pose,
While daisies debate, nobody knows!

The dandelions sing of dreams in the breeze,
Of fluffy seeds flying with such ease.
Oh, the lilacs chuckle, casting their smell,
As petals plot pranks, 'Let's cast our spell!'

The Burrows' Secret Life

In tunnels deep, the laughter flows,
As rabbits share secrets no flower knows.
A badger snoozes through all the ruckus,
Dreaming of carrots and meals so luscious.

While voles exchange tales, exaggerated flair,
Of daring escapes and the best hidden lair.
The clover is witness to all of their schemes,
As shadows giggle and tumble in dreams.

The Enchanted Glade

In the glade where fairies dance,
A squirrel wore a spiffy pants.
With acorn hats and shoes that squeak,
They giggled loud for quite a week.

Mushrooms sing and flowers sway,
While frogs leap high in their ballet.
The gnomes argue over great big pies,
As butterflies play tag in the skies.

A rabbit makes a witty pun,
'Why chase the sun? I'm having fun!'
His friends all chuckle with delight,
In this glade, all worries take flight.

So when you wander, take a chance,
You might just join the forest dance.
In laughter, joy, and playful cheer,
You'll find a world that's pure and clear.

Ferns and Fantasies

Ferns are swaying, dressed in green,
Whispering secrets, oh so keen.
A hedgehog dreams of pizza pie,
While ants in line begin to cry.

A rabbit juggles nuts and seeds,
He's quite the star, fulfilling needs.
While owls debate who sings the best,
In the moonlight, they take their rest.

Tiny fairies trade their shoes,
For sparkly hats of fuchsia blues.
They giggle as they flit and fly,
As clouds drift lazily in the sky.

In this place of joyful games,
Where laughter flows and nothing's tame,
Come join the ferns, don't be shy,
In this dreamy realm, let spirits fly.

A Tapestry of Twigs

Twigs are woven, oh so fine,
Creating art, a grand design.
A raccoon wears a stylish tie,
As chipmunks cheer and squirrels fly.

They build their castles from the ground,
Where silly sounds are all around.
With wobbly legs, a fawn joins in,
Wearing a crown made of an old tin.

In sticky mud, the frogs reside,
Creating masterpieces worldwide.
They paint their dreams in shades of green,
And giggle at the things they've seen.

A tapestry unfolds so bright,
In this safe haven, pure delight.
With jokes and pranks, it's all in fun,
Under the gaze of a warming sun.

Birdsong and Moonlight

In moonlit nights, the birds confer,
With tipsy tunes from every spur.
A whip-poor-will spills tea with flair,
While crickets cheer from everywhere.

A parrot sporting shades so bold,
Tells tales of treasures yet untold.
While owls hoot out the latest news,
Even bats join in for giggling, too.

Beetles wear a team jersey,
As grasshoppers try to be flirty.
With every chirp and rumbling sound,
This silver night is unbound.

So if you wander through this scene,
You'll find joy, and that's serene.
With melodies that make hearts sing,
In nature's choir, let laughter ring.

The Dance of Dappled Sunlight

In the forest, lights do twirl,
Sunbeams laugh, and shadows whirl.
A squirrel winks, with acorn treat,
He does a jig, with tiny feet.

Beneath the trees, the rabbits hop,
They're doing flips, oh please, don't stop!
A fox appears, all sly and spry,
He joins the fun, oh my, oh my!

The flowers giggle, petals shake,
One blooms up, and then a quake!
The beetles break into a jam,
As bugs declare, "We're all a fam!"

And as the day begins to end,
The critters laugh, and all descend.
The forest floor, that lively stage,
Is where we find the heart of play!

Enchanted Hollow: A Nature's Tale

In a glade where mushrooms glow,
A hedgehog dons a hat of snow.
With tiny shoes, he prances near,
Spreading joy, with no one fear.

A wise old owl starts to croon,
Singing to the bright, round moon.
The rabbits chuckle, wiggle their ears,
As fireflies join with giggles and cheers.

The flowers dance with vines so spry,
Dandelions wink as they float by.
A cheeky crow drops twigs and leaves,
Saying, "Let's make hats for thieves!"

In this hollow, tricks are grand,
Nature's laughter fills the land.
Each creature joins with gleeful shouts,
In this place where fun sprouts out!

Murmurs from the Burbling Brook

The brook hums tunes, all slap and splash,
Where fish wag tales of a daring dash.
A frog leaps high, quite full of glee,
Says, "Look at me! I'm fancy-free!"

The dragonflies buzz, their wings all bright,
Chasing each other, such a funny sight.
Weaving and swirling, they dance in pairs,
Like tiny pilots, soaring through airs.

A duck quacks jokes beneath the reeds,
While turtles snore, ignoring the leads.
The water tickles the edges wide,
As laughter spreads, like a joyful tide!

In this lively stream, the chatter flows,
With every ripple, the laughter grows.
So if you hear a splash and croak,
Just know it's fun that the brook bespoke!

Shadows of Ancient Oaks

Under oaks so grand and wise,
The critter clans plot their surprise.
A raccoon wears a crown of leaves,
As midnight snacks are what he believes.

A hedgehog spins a yarn or two,
While chipmunks gather, planning their brew.
With friends so clever and so spry,
They sneak through shadows, oh my, oh my!

Each branch above, a stage so vast,
Where squirrels perform, quite unsurpassed.
The nuts they toss create a ruckus,
A woodland circus, none could duck us!

The night's alive with merry sounds,
As laughter echoes 'round and 'round.
In these shadows, joy's the key,
Where every friend can truly be free!

The Treasure of Dew-Kissed Petals

Amidst the blooms, the ants parade,
With tiny hats, they waltz and sway.
A ladybug joins, in her high-top shoes,
They laugh and giggle as they dance and cruise.

A rabbit hops by, with a curious glance,
He trips on his ears, but still wants to prance.
The flowers all giggle, their petals aglow,
As he tumbles and rolls, putting on a show.

A bumblebee buzzes, with a cupcake crown,
Proudly he flits, never wearing a frown.
He offers sweet nectar to everyone there,
While butterflies flutter in colorful air.

At twilight they gather, a festival bright,
With dew-kissed petals that shimmer in light.
They share tales of mischief, from all through the day,
In this quirky garden, where giggles hold sway.

Serenade of the Moonlit Thicket

In shadows of trees, the frogs start to croak,
They're juggling fireflies, a comical folk.
A raccoon arrives with a bandit's grin,
Singing of snacks he might find in a bin.

The owls hoot in rhythm, a gossiping crew,
While crickets provide a loud beat, it's true.
They chirp about humans and their funny ways,
As the moon beams down on their starry displays.

A fox in a tuxedo struts down the lane,
With a dapper demeanor and no hint of shame.
He tips his top hat and bows with a flair,
For all of his friends, who giggle and stare.

As dawn starts to break, their sonata concludes,
The thicket falls silent, it's tired of moods.
But in dreams, they'll dance to a moonlit refrain,
In the heart of the forest, where fun's never plain.

Beneath the Tangle of Vines

Tangled in green, a squirrel takes a leap,
He lands on a branch, but can't find his feet.
He rolls and he tumbles, with grace like a cat,
While a nearby crow caws, "Well, how about that?"

A snail on the ground wears a crown made of leaves,
Dreaming of races, while everyone grieves.
"I'll win when I'm ready!" he boldly proclaims,
As the other bugs chuckle, all calling him names.

A beetle with shades lounges on a log,
Sipping on raindrops, he's a chill kind of frog.
He throws a pool party for all of his pals,
"Bring your best snacks!" he shouts to the gals.

When the sun starts to set, the laughter erupts,
They share silly stories, all giggles and ups.
Beneath tangled vines, in a world full of cheer,
These critters all gather, their fun they hold dear.

Reflections in a Crystal Pool

A duck with a hat struts along the shore,
Practicing quacks, while he makes quite the score.
His friends start to join, with floats and balloons,
They splash in the water, beneath the cool moons.

The fish swim in circles, a synchronized crew,
Wearing tiny tuxedos, oh what a view!
They wiggle and giggle, their scales flash and gleam,
Creating a whirlpool, it's all like a dream.

A frog with a flute leads a musical band,
While turtles tap dance on the silty, wet sand.
The reeds sway along, like they're caught in a trance,
As the critters all join in, a wild, funny dance.

As night settles down, the stars twinkle bright,
They gather their stories and share pure delight.
Reflections ripple gently, as laughter takes flight,
In this crystal-clear pool, where all feels just right.

The Hollow's Call

In the tree's embrace, a squirrel sighs,
With acorns aplenty, a feast he spies.
Yet, when he jumps, he slips and falls,
And lands right where the porcupine sprawls.

The wise old owl, with a chuckle, hoots,
As the squirrel dances in funny flutes.
He tries to impress on the forest stage,
But ends up tangled in a shoelace rage.

The rabbits chuckle as they hop nearby,
While the fox pretends he's shooting for the sky.
In the hollow, laughter's a daily call,
As critters unite for the humorous brawl.

Oh, the bumbles and tumbles of forest fun,
Where everyone's silly, under the sun.
In nature's own comedy, all take a part,
With laughter and joy, wrapped in woodland art.

Sunbeams through the Treetops

A sunbeam slips through, tickling a deer,
Who's trying to nap but can't quite cheer.
With a bounce and a twist, she leaps to her feet,
Chasing the shadows, a dancing retreat.

The chipmunks prance, playing tag with the light,
While the old tortoise grumbles, 'It's too bright tonight!'
But with sunshine and laughter, all have their say,
As they join in a warm and giggly ballet.

A butterfly flutters, wearing a crown,
While ants in a line march all the way down.
They trip on a twig, fall back in a heap,
And then burst out laughing, abandoning sleep.

The treetops giggle as the day goes along,
In a forest so lively, where all sing a song.
With sunbeams and joy, and funny bunches,
Every corner's a stage for silly little munches.

Nurtured by Nature's Hand

A hedgehog stumbles, going for a stroll,
With a picnic basket, he's on a roll.
But in his excitement, he tumbles and fumbles,
And sends his snacks flying, oh how he grumbles!

The trees just chuckle, swaying in mirth,
As out of nowhere, a raccoon gives birth -
To a whole lot of laughter, as her cubs chase a bee,
Buzzing by clumsily, as busy as can be.

With fruits and nuts raining from over the boughs,
The critters all gather, some even say 'Wow!'
Pickles and berries, all rolled in a line,
Creating a banquet that's simply divine.

Yet through it all, in their quirky dance,
Each woodland creature takes a silly chance.
With nature's embrace, they thrive in the play,
Funny mishaps brighten their sunny day.

Ramble Through the Underbrush

In the underbrush thick, a rabbit sneezes loud,
Startling the turtles, who shyly scowl proud.
With a flick of a paw, she hops in surprise,
While the turtles just grin, calling it a 'wise'!

A caterpillar rolls, trying to climb,
But gets stuck on a leaf, what a comical rhyme!
He wriggles and giggles, a wiggly spree,
While the ants just march, laughing at the spree.

A deer with her fawn chases after a fly,
But slips on the dew, sending them both high.
They land in a patch of dandelion fluff,
And giggles erupt, oh, isn't that tough?

With the sun shining down, all jokes get a cheer,
In the underbrush, happiness draws near.
With mischief and laughter, nature aligns,
In a tangled up world where comedy shines.

Embracing the Silence of Pine Needles

Underneath the tall, green dome,
Pine needles whisper secrets, all alone.
Squirrels chatter, plotting their cheer,
While a frog croaks out, 'I'm outta here!'

Raindrops tickle, a game of hide and seek,
A chipmunk giggles, oh so sleek.
Beneath the boughs, shadows dance and play,
Nature's stand-up show, every day.

In the stillness, laughter echoes wide,
Even the oaks can't help but chide.
With roots that wiggle, and branches that sway,
Each moment here, it's pure cabaret!

So join the fun where the pine trees stand,
Grab a nut, maybe a clover strand.
Let's laugh with the leaves, let joy unfurl,
In this secret world, just give it a twirl.

The Legacy of Gnarled Roots

Twisted roots tell stories of old,
Sagas of trees, both brave and bold.
A log sits grumpy, a wise old sage,
While fungi plot their next witty page.

With every curl, a tale unwinds,
Of squirrelly antics and whimsical finds.
A beetle, wearing his fanciest shoes,
Tap dances proudly, spreading the news.

The moss laughs softly, a green fluffy crown,
While acorns bounce like they're going to town.
With every knock, the forest replies,
Nature's comedy show under bright skies.

So heed the roots, gnarled and wise,
In their embrace, true laughter lies.
Join the revelry, sing your tune,
In this bark-clad circus, under the moon.

Whimsical Tales of the Forest Floor

Leaves tumble down in a giggling spree,
Caterpillars dance, as happy as can be.
Mushrooms wear hats in colors so bright,
An owl hoots, 'What a marvelous sight!'

Distance echoes with a chuckling breeze,
Crickets chirp jokes with unsteady ease.
A ladybug flirts, shares a wink with a bee,
While ants march by with a grand jubilee.

Sticks become swords in a woodland play,
Where every creature finds joy in the sway.
Beneath the tall ferns, a treasure hunt brews,
For acorns and laughter, there's never a snooze.

So gather 'round, hear the stories unfold,
As the forest floor brims with laughter untold.
In this carnival of wonders, join the fun,
In every nook, there's joy for everyone!

Wings Among the Canopy

High above, the chirps and flutters,
Birds debate in comic mutters.
A parrot preens in bright ensemble,
While owls roll eyes, in wise dissemble.

Fluttering banners in russet and gold,
Hummingbirds zip, never too old.
A jay tells jokes, with a raucous squawk,
While squirrels jump from tree to block.

In the branches, a party never ends,
Where feathery pals are all good friends.
A whimsical waltz among leafy eaves,
In laughter's arms, the heart believes.

So let us soar, light as a song,
In the canopy's giggles, we all belong.
With wings and whimsy, our spirits soar,
Each fluttering tale leaves us wanting more.

Lanterns of the Fireflies

In the night the bugs do buzz,
With tiny lights that give a fuzz.
They dance around in silly shoes,
A glowing party in the dewy hues.

The frogs are croaking like a band,
While crickets play their strings so grand.
A firefly trips over a root,
And lands right next to a snoozing brute!

They flicker bright, they twirl and spin,
Like tiny stars, they start to grin.
But watch your step, don't take a fall,
Or end up stuck in a bugball!

As dawn breaks, the dance must end,
With sleepy heads they start to blend.
The woodland wakes from snoozing deep,
While fireflies dream of their next leap.

Spirits of the Sylvan Realm

In the glen where shadows play,
Sit the spirits, strange and gay.
They juggle acorns, toss some leaves,
And laugh at all our human grieves.

A squirrel gives a valiant yell,
As gnomes backflip—what a spell!
With mushrooms worn as caps so tall,
They hold a feast, the woodland ball.

For every tree that bends and bows,
There's magic held in knobby brows.
The pixies giggle, mischief planned,
With twinkling eyes and sticky hand.

They'll prank you good, conceal your snack,
And hide your boots behind the track.
So watch your back and keep your cheer,
For woodland spirits always near!

The Thicket's Tale

Through the thorns, I trip and tumble,
Hushed whispers force me to stumble.
The hedgehogs plot a ballroom dance,
　While rabbits giggle at my chance.

A bushy tail waves in delight,
As chubby chipmunks start a fight.
With acorns flying left and right,
It's a nutty brawl from day till night!

A wise old owl gives a hoot,
While passing bees insist on loot.
With honey jars all stacked so high,
　They barter for a piece of pie!

The thicket stirs with chuckles bright,
　As nature shares its pure delight.
　Among the chaos and the cheer,
　A glimpse of joy is always near.

Roots in Reverie

Beneath the tree, the roots do twist,
A tangled mess where fairies tryst.
They sip on dew, and giggle low,
In nature's nook, with tools to stow.

A hedgehog sports a leafy crown,
While headstands make the daisies frown.
The mushrooms laugh with jolly glee,
As rabbits blend in with the spree.

With each fine root a tale unfolds,
Of wild adventures, bold and bold.
They disguise themselves in silly dress,
And challenge all to a light-hearted guess!

In playful whispers, secrets bloom,
Among the roots, there's always room.
For laughter rings in vibrant strands,
And dreams come true in gentle hands.

Mood of the Murmuring Brook

The brook has giggles, bubbling loud,
Fish in tuxedos, all so proud.
A frog with a crown leaps on a log,
He claims he's the king, but he's just a bog.

Ducks wear hats, quacking in verse,
Each splash a rumor, each wave diverse.
They trade their tales of summer fun,
While sipping on tea, under the sun.

The pebbles gossip about travels far,
One thinks he's a diamond, a real superstar.
But slipped from a pocket, he's back with the sand,
Dreaming of glories, but never so grand.

So down by the brook, laughter cascades,
Where the water's a joker, never afraid.
In rippling rhythms, the stories unfold,
Of fishy adventures and treasures untold.

Constellations in the Canopy

Look up above, there's a squirrel brigade,
Mapping the stars while munching on shade.
They point with their paws at a peanut-shaped moon,
Planning their travels with a nutty cartoon.

Leaves shimmy down, tickling our cheeks,
While birds tell secrets in chirpy squeaks.
A wise old owl nods, wearing spectacles wide,
He's the cosmic librarian of our leafy slide.

A raccoon crafts tales from twigs and bark,
Each sentence a riddle, a joke, or a quark.
constellations made of snacks are divine,
With marshmallow clouds and candy cane vines.

So don't be surprised by the laughter above,
Nature's a jester, and we're all in love.
When the night drapes softly, and the stars start to twinkle,
The canopy giggles, and dreams start to sprinkle.

The Mystery of the Maidenhair

In the hush of the grove, where shadows prance,
The maidenhair whispers, inviting a glance.
She tells silly secrets to trees and the breeze,
Of squirrels in tutus, swaying with ease.

Fluffy ferns dance, all dressed in green,
They gossip of mushrooms, their neighborly teen.
A ladybug winks, with spots galore,
Claiming she's fancy, and so much more.

The sunlight chuckles as it flickers by,
Caressing the leaves, while the crickets comply.
In this curious realm where laughter does bloom,
Even the fungi wear hats filled with gloom.

So wander awhile, let joy be your guide,
As the mystery unfolds in the roots and the stride.
In every leaf's shimmer, a jest is portrayed,
In the heart of the maidenhair, fun is displayed.

Celebrating the Twisted Roots

Roots that twist like a dancer's shoe,
Waltzing through soil, with a whimsical view.
They wiggle and giggle, a tangled delight,
Sharing old stories of how they took flight.

The gnarled oak laughs, a wise granddad tree,
With branches so shaky, he giggles with glee.
"Once I was sprightly, up high in the sky,
Now I'm just grounded, watching clouds float by."

Vines weave a tale, of rambles and rolls,
Entwining their paths, making up silly goals.
"Let's grow to the moon, we'll swing with a band,
Play music with leaves, and twirl on the sand!"

So here's to the roots that rumble in jest,
With laughter and mischief, they truly are blessed.
In the heart of the earth, where craziness steeps,
The dance of the roots, where humor still leaps.

Echoes of the Forest Floor

Squirrels chatter, planning their feast,
A raccoon rummages, looking for sweets.
Foxes' laughter echoes in the air,
While deer just glance, with a devil-may-care.

Mushrooms dance in their polka-dot hats,
While rabbits debate which way to scat.
The owls hoot jokes from their tree so tall,
As crickets chirp, saying, 'We're having a ball!'

Frogs tell tales from the murky old creek,
About a turtle who thought he could sneak.
They ribbit and giggle, their truth hard to find,
As the wind carries laughter of every kind.

In this delightful nook, where oddball ideas,
Float like lost socks in the soft summer breeze.
Nature's a clown, wearin' leaves as a tie,
And here in the woods, everyone's shy.

Secrets in the Shade

In shadows deep, where the critters play,
A chipmunk tells tales of the grand buffet.
With acorn crowns and a dance so spry,
They pause for a selfie—oh my, oh my!

The trees whisper secrets of squirrels in flight,
As hedgehogs complain 'bout their quills not quite right.
A wise old owl thinks he's quite the hoot,
Who knew branches could hold such a funny old brute?

Beneath the leaves where the sunlight peeks,
A party unfolds, with nature's high squeaks.
The caterpillars groove to a tiny beat,
While ants drop confetti—what a sneak peek!

With laughter that tickles both roots and the sky,
These whimsies of shade might just make you cry.
So put on your giggles and skip on the floor,
For every oak has humor galore!

Dance of the Dappled Light

Sunlight winks through the leaves above,
As shadows play games, it's a dance of love.
The butterflies swirl in a bright ballet,
While the bees hum tunes, buzzing all the way.

A ladybug joins, but trips on a stump,
The beetles all giggle, giving her a bump.
The stream keeps time with a splish and a splash,
And even the pebbles begin to dash!

In this bright arena of nature's delight,
A spider weaves patterns that sparkle just right.
With whispers of joy in the rustling leaves,
The woodland is chuckling, even while it breathes.

So grab all your friends for the grandest show,
With twirls and with giggles, let's all steal the glow!
For in this great dance beneath the sun's might,
Laughter's the magic that makes it feel right.

The Heartbeat of Moss

Moss tickles toes on the forest's soft bed,
A frog on a lily, pops jokes in your head.
With each little bounce, he goes ribbit and croak,
As shadows roll over, it's all one big joke.

An earthworm wriggles, the ground is his stage,
He narrates the stories of every old age.
With a wiggle and jiggle, he's the star of the show,
While snails slow dance with their gooey, smooth flow.

The mushrooms nod off, in their cap-twirled dream,
While ants form a line, marching, how they gleam!
Each keeps a secret, a silly old stash,
Of all the good jokes in a mossy old flash.

So listen closely, let the laughter take flight,
In the heartbeat of moss, where the joy feels just right.
For in this green haven, with giggles that spark,
Nature's a comedian, lighting up the dark.

Adventures in the Arboreal

Beneath the boughs, I saw a squirrel,
Sporting a hat and a twirl.
He danced on branches, spun with glee,
Chasing his tail, just like a spree.

A rabbit popped up, with shoes so bright,
Declared it was a fancy dress night.
They waltzed through leaves, a wacky show,
With acorns clapping—what a fun flow!

An owl hooted, wearing glasses chic,
Said, "I've read books, come take a peek!"
With puns in the air and laughter in stride,
The forest was giggling, what a wild ride!

As I wandered, I heard a frog croak,
In a tuxedo, he shared a joke.
"Why did the chicken cross the creek?
To see me in my suit—wasn't it sleek?"

Nurtured by Nature's Whispers

A raccoon cooked stew on a rock,
With mushrooms and herbs—quite a shock!
He served it up with a toothy grin,
"Hope you like it—don't ask what's in!"

The trees giggled, leaves in a flurry,
As a hedgehog raced by, oh what a hurry!
He tripped on a root, made quite a mess,
Laughed off his tumble with utmost finesse!

A ladybug dressed like a chauffeur,
Drove ants to the ball—they felt like super!
With style and flair, they rolled on by,
On a tiny leaf, oh my, oh my!

The breeze brought tales from the bees,
"Watch out for bears who steal your keys!"
Buzzing with laughter, they zipped around,
In this merry place, joy knows no bound!

The Grail of the Garden

In a patch of blooms, a gnome tried to bake,
But ended up covered in icing and cake!
With sprinkles as stars, and frosting as grass,
He pondered if plants would give him a pass.

A butterfly fluttered, all dressed in blue,
Critiqued his technique with much to pursue.
"Perhaps a soufflé, instead of a pie?
Or stick to your duties—just give it a try!"

An old tortoise came by with a snicker,
Said, "You really should work on your sticker!"
He carried a jar full of buzzing delights,
Ice cream for all on these sunny nights.

The blooms held a party, with laughter anew,
The clang of the pans and clinking of dew.
In this whimsical space, joy flew like a kite,
Where strange cook-offs sparked every night!

The Palette of the Pines

Among the pines, a painter stood,
With brushes made of twigs and mud.
He swirled the colors from nature's skin,
Creating a portrait of a cheeky grin!

A porcupine posed, all spikes and flair,
Declared, "I want to be a bear!"
With a wig of moss and a tutu bright,
He twirled in circles, oh what a sight!

A chipmunk chimed in with a jaunty song,
Said, "Join my band, it won't take long!"
With acorns as drums, they played with zest,
In the heart of the woods, they danced with the best!

As night fell down, a twilight parade,
With fireflies leading, mischief they made.
In the palette of pines, laughter soared high,
Where every creature could reach for the sky!

The Symphony of Rustling Leaves

In the breeze, the leaves do chatter,
Squirrels dance, round and round like a platter.
A raccoon with a hat, all dressed in style,
Claims he's the king, at least for a while.

A bunny hops by, with a wink and a grin,
Says he's got secrets from the great trash bin!
The laughter of crickets fills up the air,
While owls roll their eyes at the antics they share.

A chipmunk recites jokes, though he's not that good,
Trying to brighten the mood like he should.
The sun sets low, casting glimmers of gold,
And all join in laughter, young and old.

What a concert of nature, so loud and so proud,
With each rustling leaf, they gather a crowd.
So here's to the antics that nature will spin,
A symphony of joy, let the fun times begin!

Beneath the Mossy Reverie

Under a blanket of soft, mossy green,
A frog tries to croak like a queen on a screen.
But his croaks just come out as a rather strange joke,
Leaving all the critters in fits, oh what a bloke!

A snail with a shell that's a tad out of date,
Says he'll win the race, while he's still second-rate.
"A little more patience!" he says with a cheer,
"I'll catch up one day, just you wait, my dear!"

The shadows of mushrooms sway to the beat,
As ants form a line in their search for a treat.
Beneath all the giggles, the laughter runs free,
It's a party, you see, in the land of the bee!

As twilight approaches, the fun will not cease,
With tree stumps as chairs, they feast on a piece.
A festival of joy beneath mossy delight,
Where everything silly makes the world feel just right!

Dreams of a Wildflower Meadow

In a field of colors, a butterfly flits,
While a ladybug giggles, laughing at fits.
They have tea with daisies, such posh little chats,
Discussing the style of the latest green hats.

A bumblebee buzzes, all busy and bright,
But he trips on a petal, oh what a sight!
"Don't worry," they say, "it's just part of the fun,
We'll help you back up; no harm's done, my pun!"

Tall sunflowers nod, like they've had too much sun,
While dance-offs commence, oh they jump, twist, and run.

The wind carries laughter that tickles the toes,
As they twirl in the breeze, striking funny poses.

At dusk, they all gather for a giggly goodnight,
Sharing wild tales 'til the stars shine so bright.
In dreams of the meadow, where mischief takes flight,
Every flower holds laughter; what a magical sight!

Twilight Conversations with the Trees

Under the cover of dimming light,
The trees gather 'round for a chat full of fright.
"A ghost in the branches!" a pine tree will yell,
But it's just a bat, who's laughing as well.

An oak tells a tale of its youth, oh so bold,
How acorns were lost, then stumbled upon gold!
The birch with a chuckle joins in with a joke,
"Why did the twig cross the road? Just to poke!"

With rustling branches, they share silly fears,
Of swaying in storms, and too many cheers.
The shadows grow long, and they hoot and they howl,
As breezy banter fills up the night and the soil.

And as the moon peeks, their laughter stays bright,
With trees telling stories, what a marvelous sight!
So here's to their tales, in the crunch of the leaves,
A playful collection of what nature believes.

Whispers of the Leafy Canopy

Up high, the branches shake with glee,
Squirrels play poker, oh what a spree!
The acorns are betting with all their might,
They giggle and wiggle, what a wild sight!

A chattering chipmunk joins in the fun,
He juggles pinecones—what a skillful run!
With every small slip, the laughter erupts,
As nature's own circus continues and jumps!

The owls roll their eyes, so wise and aloof,
They wonder who's hosting this nutty goof.
The leaves rustle secrets, a leafy ballet,
Where whimsy and joy lead the frolicsome play!

In shadows of green, the laughter floats high,
A world full of antics beneath the blue sky!
So raise up your juice, your snacks on a tray,
To the woodland shindig—let's dance all day!

Secrets Beneath the Tall Pines

Beneath the tall pines, a snail takes a stroll,
Wearing a backpack, he's got quite a goal!
He dreams of the leaves at the end of the lane,
Yet slugs pass him by, honking horns in disdain.

A gopher, quite clever, is brewing some tea,
With dandelion sprigs—oh, what a spree!
He's invited the critters to share in his brew,
But they're all too busy with antics askew!

The rabbits are jumping like they just found a find,
While ants are playing tag, they're so hard to bind!
With wiggles and giggles, it's true they conspire,
To pull the big pine cone and start a choir!

And when dusk falls gently, they'll gather and sing,
To honor the laughter that wildness can bring.
So if you wander past, don't be shy, come near,
To join in the laughter of nature sincere!

Echoes in the Fern-Laden Glade

In the glade where ferns nestle down by the creek,
A fox wears a hat, it's quite the mystique!
He jives with the shadows, a smooth sailor's dance,
Leaving the rabbits to giggle and prance!

The turtle joins in, with his own tambourine,
With every soft tap, he shows off his sheen.
The critters all cheer, what a sight to behold,
As secrets of laughter through foliage unfold!

A butterfly flutters, puts on a show,
With twirls and with spins, where could she go?
The bumblebees buzz, they're singing a tune,
To a beat that's played by a jazzy raccoon!

In the heart of the glade, where oddities live,
The whispers of fun seem eternally give.
So next time you wander, come gather the cheer,
For laughter is currency, worth more than mere deer!

Starlit Paths and Unseen Trails

On starlit paths where shadows weave,
A hedgehog rides bikes, oh can you believe?
He toots on a horn, joined by a raccoon,
Both zooming along to a well-timed tune!

With treats made of berries, they stop for a feast,
Inviting the owls, the funniest beast!
With marshmallows flying and fires aglow,
They roast all their snacks while putting on a show!

The twinkling of stars sends giggles through trees,
As creatures unite with a rustling breeze.
They trade silly stories, each funnier still,
In the moonlit embrace, they're wild and fulfilled!

So when night comes calling, just follow the sound,
For laughter and fun are the treasures abound.
Join in with the critters, partake in their way,
For nighttime's the time where adventures can play!

The Call of the Timberland

In the heart of the trees, the squirrels conspire,
They plot little pranks, fueled by leafy desire.
A brave chipmunk stands guard, with a nut for a sword,
Defending his hoard from a roguish old horde.

The owls hoot with laughter, their eyes all aglow,
As they watch the chipmunk put on quite a show.
With acorns as missiles, the battle ignites,
A fairytale war 'neath the starry night sights.

Whispering Willows

The willows are gossiping, bending with glee,
"Did you see that rabbit? He tripped over a bee!"
They chuckle and sway, sharing tales of the day,
As the groundhogs roll by in a comical way.

The frogs join the fray, croaking tunes on the shore,
Mimicking the loons with a ribbit encore.
The rustling leaves join in, chiming softly, they tease,
It's a woodland revue, with sass and a breeze.

Sunlit Shadows

In the dazzle of sunlight, the shadows all play,
Making shapes of odd creatures that dance and sway.
A shadow of a moose winks at a passing hare,
With a flick of its antlers, they giggle in air.

Nearby, a fat beetle attempts to jig,
While a crabapple falls with an ungraceful squig.
The berries all blush as they bounce and they roll,
In a sun-drenched spectacle that tickles the soul.

The Stillness of the Stump

On the stump in the glade, a raccoon sets scene,
With a treasure of snacks fit for a cheeky cuisine.
The chipmunks are munching, a feast on the lawn,
While a turtle jumps in with a splash... and a yawn.

With the stillness of silence, the laughter erupts,
As the critters convene, their silliness erupts.
The skies echo giggles, a raucous delight,
In the heart of the forest, where levity's bright.

The Stillness Between Raindrops

Raindrops dance and play their game,
Jumping puddles, oh what a fame!
A squirrel slips, a boisterous shout,
Splashes fly, oh watch them pout!

In the bushes, a frog in a hat,
Croaking news, just look at that!
He claims he's king of the wet parade,
But slips and slides, oh what a charade!

Trees whisper secrets, hushed and sly,
The wind-tickled leaves laugh, oh my!
Nature giggles, it's quite a show,
With each little droplet, a merry flow!

The sun peeks out for a quick surprise,
Painting rainbows that twist and rise.

The Tangle of Thorns

In the garden, what a mess,
A thicket of thorns in an awful dress!
Curly vines wrap around my shoes,
Sneaky little creepers, oh what a ruse!

Bumbling bees buzz in a fuss,
Hitching rides on a clumsy bus.
I swat and flail in a thorny gale,
Each prick a tickle, I can't prevail!

A hedgehog giggles and rolls away,
I blame him for this thorny play.
With every step, I make a shout,
Nature's pranksters, no doubt about!

Finally free, but what a scene,
Thorns in my hair, looking quite mean.
I'll guard my treasures, that's for sure,
Next time I'll wear armor for this tour!

Waking the Wildflowers

Down in the glen, they're snoozing tight,
Wildflowers dreaming of morning light.
I tiptoe close with a silly grin,
"Time to rise up, let's go for a spin!"

With a gentle poke, a dandelion yawns,
Says, "Not yet, please, I'm counting the dawns!"
A poppy pouts, "Oh, stay in bed!"
But I shake my head, this is what I said!

"Come on, dear blooms! The sun's on the way!"
"Coffee or tea?" one daisy did sway.
"Maybe a latte, with froth on the top!"
They giggled and swayed, a bright flowery hop!

At last they wake, each one in a tune,
Dancing with joy, under the moon.
Nature's party now bursts into cheer,
As all the wildflowers shout, "We're here!"

The Myth of the Moonlit Clearing

Beneath the moon, a tale unfolds,
Of nimble sprites and brave-hearted folds.
They claim the night is theirs to hold,
With twinkling lights, oh so bold.

A hedgehog winks, "I'm in on the joke!"
As giggles rise from the midnight cloak.
Witty fairies play tricks on the trees,
Whispering secrets on the soft breeze.

"Oh look!" says one, "A startled owl!"
"Why's he scowling with that frowning scowl?"
The moon beams bright, like a spotlight show,
On the whimsy of creatures in adorable flow!

But lo and behold, as dawn starts to peek,
The sprites scurry fast, in a playful streak.
Leaving behind a glimmering trail,
Of laughter and mischief, a magical tale!

Invocations of the Ivy

In the corner, ivy climbs,
Scratching walls in silly rhymes.
A whispered joke, a leafy grin,
Wonders bloom where tunes begin.

Squirrels chatter, acorns fly,
One popped up, oh my, oh my!
A twist of fate and nature's jest,
Laughing leaves, we are all blessed.

Beneath the boughs, a critter plays,
Swings on vines like silly rays.
He stops to munch on fledgling snacks,
Oh, to be a vine-bound ax!

The ivy chuckles in the breeze,
With every sway, it tries to tease.
"Join us now, let's dance and twirl!"
In the green, the fun unfurls.

Bough's Embrace

The branches hug, a leafy cheer,
Telling tales for all to hear.
A lively dance of shadowed fun,
Where every bark's a prank begun.

A robin trips, then strikes a pose,
On a branch, he strikes a nose.
With goofy hops and flaps so bold,
Nature's laughter never gets old.

Beneath the shade, the critters plot,
A game of chase, a tangled knot.
The sun peeks in, a playful spy,
"Catch them quick!" the whispers fly.

In every twist, a giggle lies,
In every rustle, laughter flies.
Oh, how we celebrate and play,
In this embracing, leafy fray.

The Echoes of Enchanted Echoes

Whispers bounce through forest halls,
Playful echoes, giggling calls.
Before you know it, trees start to tease,
In merry tunes, they strive to please.

A hare hops back to join the sound,
Thumping feet, they gather 'round.
With every leap, another joke,
The trees laugh loud, the branches poke.

Old owls chuckle, wise and bright,
"Why did the crow take flight tonight?"
They tell their tales beneath the moon,
Echoes linger, a funny tune.

The forest giggles, all in sync,
As shadows dance, we laugh and wink.
In this place where echoes grow,
We find the joy of nature's show.

The Dawn of Dewy Dances

Morning blushes, dew drops spark,
The world awakes, a lark's remark.
With nimble feet, the flowers sway,
Dancing bright to greet the day.

A bunny leaps, a clumsy twirl,
Stumbling here, and there, a whirl.
The bees buzz low, a tiny cheer,
In this bright morn, no room for fear.

With each first ray, the critters grin,
Their twirling tails like whirling pins.
Together in this sunlit trance,
Each petal adds to nature's dance.

Laughter rises with the sun,
In this ballet, we all have fun.
Every drop of dew's a chance,
To join the joyful, dewy dance.

The Hidden Magic of Ferns

Beneath the fronds, the fairies play,
In leafy hats, they whittle away.
Their giggles spill like morning dew,
While rabbits sneak a peek or two.

A squirrel gets tangled in a vine,
Declares, "I'm just a dancer, fine!"
But tripping over roots so spry,
He blames the ferns and makes them cry.

The dappled light begins to sway,
As shadow sprites come out to play.
They hide behind the curling leaves,
Crafting mischief that deceives.

To catch a glimpse of what they do,
One must wear ferns as hats too!
With ferns like crowns and joy so wide,
Nature's jesters dance with pride.

Glimpses of Faery Footprints

In mossy glades, a path appears,
With tiny shoes and many cheers.
A bumblebee begins to buzz,
As footstep prints lead where it does.

A line of ants in single file,
Think they're traveling in style.
But faeries twist their tiny toes,
As giggles travel where no one goes.

The toadstools nod and hats tip low,
"Who left these prints?" the squirrels crow.
A trail of glitter, hops, and skips,
Encourages a dance of flips!

Keep watch and listen by the stream,
Where cutting jokes and laughter gleam.
For faery fun is hard to spot,
Unless you're looking for the plot!

The Lure of Forgotten Paths

A winding trail through tangled grass,
Where every creature stops to pass.
A hedgehog smirks, a turtle blinks,
And echoes carry secret links.

An ancient gate swings wide, yet creaks,
As rabbits take their daring leaps.
They hop and giggle, plot and play,
As if they own the grand café.

A snaky root declares a dare,
Who'll climb the highest, who'll beware?
Amidst the herbs and scents so sweet,
A game unwinds, a quirky treat.

Yet wander not too far away,
For squirrels might steal your lunch today.
Their paws are quick, their tricks abound,
In every nook where fun is found!

Twilight Secrets of the Birch Grove

As daylight fades to shades of grey,
The birches whisper, "Come and play!"
With silver bark that shimmers bright,
They tell of laughter in the night.

A fox with flair takes center stage,
Recites his lines upon the page.
The owls hoot rhythm, bats take flight,
As shadows wiggle, bringing light.

Sprightly sprites in gleaming gowns,
Sprinkle joy on sleepy towns.
Unearthly giggles fill the air,
While twirling in their moonlit lair.

So come beneath the silver trees,
And join the dance that sways with ease.
For in this grove of twilight fame,
Each creature here has found a name.

Fern Fronds and Fables

In the shade where ferns do grow,
A mushroom dressed in morning glow.
It tells tales to passersby,
Of squirrels in suits who love to fly.

The fox in boots struts with flair,
While rabbits giggle without a care.
An acorn hat upon his head,
He hops and hopes for berry bread.

The owl plays chess with a wise old toad,
Who claims he knows a secret road.
But when it rains, they slip and slide,
Across the grass, their laughter wide.

In ferny groves, we find delight,
As laugh-filled days turn into night.
With whimsy in every nook and bend,
These fables shared will never end.

The Melodies of Mossy Stones

Beneath the rocks, the tiny crickets sing,
While snails play tunes on a leafy string.
With every note, the mushrooms dance,
A frolicsome feast, a wild romance.

The stones wear hats of emerald green,
They gossip and giggle, a merry scene.
Each mossy patch a stage for fun,
As ants parade under the sun.

The ladybug laughs at her own small size,
Wearing a crown made of fireflies.
With citrus shades and glimmering rays,
She twirls and swirls in summer's haze.

When twilight falls, the tunes still play,
With night critters joining the cabaret.
Mossy stones hum, their laughter bright,
As we drift away on dreams of night.

Dreams of the Deer

In moonlit glades, the deer do prance,
Wearing flower crowns in a fanciful dance.
They twirl and leap, oh what a sight,
With butterflies spinning, hearts taking flight.

One curious fawn with a comical face,
Tripped on a twig, oh, what a place!
He rolled in laughter, his mother sighed,
But even she chuckled, with wide-open pride.

A picnic of acorns, they gathered with glee,
While raccoons plotted a food jubilee.
With berries a-plenty and snacks galore,
The merriment rang, they begged for more!

As stars twinkled bright in the moon's embrace,
The deer held a banquet, a joyous chase.
In dreams, they frolic, with hearts full and free,
In the night's gentle hush, as funny as can be.

Forest Paths and Fabled Trails

Along the path where the wildflowers bloom,
A hedgehog recites a poem to the moon.
With every word, the fireflies twinkle,
As raccoons cackle and giggles sprinkle.

The path winds like tales of yore,
With gnomes in the bushes, oh what a score!
Each step a riddle, each turn a surprise,
With pixies hiding, not very wise.

A squirrel in a cape takes flight on a breeze,
While snickering owls watch from their trees.
"Whoooo knew walks could bring such cheer?"
They hoot, as they sip their squirrel-made beer.

As laughter echoes through every bend,
The forest delights, where joy knows no end.
With fables spun from the tales of trails,
Life's a grand jest where hilarity prevails.

The Heartbeat of the Understory

In shadows deep, the critters creep,
A squirrel in shades of stylish gray.
He's caught a glance, in a funny dance,
While stealing acorns on his way.

A rabbit hops with floppy ears,
And stumbles over roots, oh dear!
With every leap, the thickets peep,
A nature show that brings us cheer.

The birds above in colorful garb,
Chase each other with chirps and caws.
They squawk and fall, oh what a brawl,
A comedy without a pause.

So here we sit, with nature's wit,
Observing antics under sun.
In laughter's thrill, we find our fill,
In this woodland where joy has run.

Ephemeral Moments in the Wild

A fox in boots, oh what a sight,
He struts with pride, a dapper knight.
In search of snacks, with swinging backs,
He stumbles on a ladybug's flight.

The owls declare with solemn flair,
Their wisdom wrapped in bedtime yawn.
But every night, they take to flight,
And swoop with shenanigans till dawn.

A dandelion dreams of being grand,
It wishes to tickle the evening breeze.
But every puff sends seeds a-stuff,
And they land where nobody sees.

So raise a cheer for moments dear,
The laughter shared in leaf and grass.
In fleeting times, with silly rhymes,
Nature's stage is where we pass.

Whispers Among the Trees

The trees are chatting, can you hear?
With gossip leaves that tickle air.
A branch does sway, to share the day,
As squirrels giggle without a care.

The chipmunks boast of secret nests,
In which they hide their fanciest treats.
In rustling glee, they dance for free,
With acorn hats that can't be beat!

A rabbit slips into the fray,
And trips right over roots so sly.
He shakes his head, then hops ahead,
As all the flora laughs awry.

Among the greens, their jokes convene,
In nature's pub where all collaborate.
With every quirk, and laughter's perk,
The forest's heart does celebrate.